HISTORY'S MOST INFLUENTIAL

# INVENTORS

# FROM THE Early 1800s TO THE Late 1800s

*Eli Whitney to Georges Leclanché*

EDITED BY ROBERT CURLEY



Britannica® Educational Publishing

IN ASSOCIATION WITH

ROSEN EDUCATIONAL SERVICES

Published in 2025 by Britannica Educational Publishing
(a trademark of Encyclopædia Britannica, Inc.)
in association with Rosen Educational Services, LLC
2544 Clinton Street, Buffalo, NY 14224.



Distributed exclusively by Rosen Educational Services.
For a listing of additional Britannica Educational Publishing titles, call toll free (800) 237-9932.

First Edition

Britannica Educational Publishing
**Michael I. Levy: Executive Editor**
Marilyn L. Barton: Senior Coordinator, Production Control
Steven Bosco: Director, Editorial Technologies
Lisa S. Braucher: Senior Producer and Data Editor
Yvette Charboneau: Senior Copy Editor
Kathy Nakamura: Manager, Media Acquisition
Robert Curley: Manager, Science and Technology

Editor: Greg Roza
Book design: Michael Flynn

Photo credits: Cover https://commons.wikimedia.org/wiki/File:Samuel_Finley_Breese_Morse_-_Samuel_F._B._Morse_Self-Portrait_-_Google_Art_Project.jpg; p. 6 Morphart Creation/Shutterstock.com; p. 17 Everett Collection/Shutterstock.com; p. 20 courtesy of the Library of Congress; p. 35 vectorfusionart/Shutterstock.com; p. 49 Timofeeff/Shutterstock.com; p. 55 https://commons.wikimedia.org/wiki/File:John_Wesley_Hyatt,_Jr.jpg; p. 58 Morphart Creation/Shutterstock.com.

**Cataloging-in-Publication Data**

Names: Curley, Robert, 1955-.
Title: From the early 1800s to the late 1800s: Eli Whitney to Georges Leclanché / edited by Robert Curley.
Description: New York : Britannica Educational Publishing, in Association with Rosen Educational Services, 2025. | Series: History's most influential inventors | Includes glossary and index.
Identifiers: ISBN 9781641900904 (library bound) | ISBN 9781641900898 (pbk) | ISBN 9781641900911 (ebook)
Subjects: LCSH: Inventors--Biography. | Inventions--History.
Classification: LCC T39.F766 2025 | DDC 609.2'2--dc23

*Manufactured in the United States of America*

CPSIA Compliance Information: Batch #CSBRIT25. For further information contact Rosen Publishing at 1-800-237-9932.

# CONTENTS

# INTRODUCTION

*"One's invention is another's tool."*
*—Samuel F. B. Morse (1791–1872)*

Life has been transformed over the years through the efforts of the men and women who had the brilliance, diligence, and creativity to come up with new and better ways of doing things. This book focuses on the inventions of people who lived in the early through late 1800s. As detailed throughout these pages, their inventions spawned many more inventions, speeding up the pace of progress even further.

These inventors clearly improved life by keeping people healthier, helping them to communicate and work more efficiently, and allowing them to travel farther. Stethoscopes, invented by René Laënnec, allowed doctors to better diagnose and treat disease and injury. The system of braille, developed by Louis Braille, made it possible for blind people to read. And George Stephenson's development of the railroad locomotive allowed passengers to cross greater distances.

However, some inventions, while having their obvious benefits, have also had their pitfalls. Before Eli Whitney invented the cotton gin, separating cotton lint from its seeds was a 10-hour, labor-intensive ordeal. Whitney's invention transformed cotton production into a rapid process that for the first time made cotton farming a highly profitable business. Yet the cotton gin also prolonged slavery, as cotton plantations needed a larger labor force to keep up with increased production demands.

Some inventions throughout history have occurred purely by accident. In an effort to find an inexpensive way to print his own plays, Austrian actor and playwright Alois

Senefelder stumbled across the promising potential of using fine-grained stone instead of copper plate, thereby inventing the process of lithography.

In 1839, businessman Charles Goodyear was looking for a way to make natural rubber more pliable, when he accidentally spilled some rubber mixed with sulfur on a hot stove. He discovered that instead of melting, the rubber became more elastic. Thus was the vulcanization process born, and with it a whole range of uses for rubber.

This book recognizes not only the inventors whose work changed the course of human life, but also those whose ideas paved the way for future generations of inventors. In the mid-1800s, mathematician Charles Babbage developed a model for an automatic computing engine, but he never built his device. A century later, Babbage's idea that a machine could perform scientific computations reemerged, and today the computer is recognized as one of the most revolutionary inventions in history.

So many inventors have made important contributions in this time period that to mention them all here would far exceed the space limitations of this book. The figures who have been included are among the greatest and most prolific inventors of all time. They were selected because their inventions have altered the course of people's lives and have left an indelible stamp on human history.

## ELI WHITNEY

(b. Dec. 8, 1765, Westboro, Mass. [now in U.S.]—d. Jan. 8, 1825, New Haven, Conn., U.S.)

Eli Whitney was an American inventor, mechanical engineer, and manufacturer, best remembered as the inventor of the cotton gin but most important for developing the concept of mass production of interchangeable parts.

Whitney's father was a respected farmer who served as a justice of the peace. In May 1789 Whitney entered Yale

*Eli Whitney's cotton gin, shown here, revolutionized the cotton industry by making it much easier to separate the cotton from the seed.*

College, where he learned many of the new concepts and experiments in science and the applied arts, as technology was then called. After graduation in the fall of 1792, Whitney was disappointed twice in promised teaching posts. The second offer was in Georgia, where, stranded without employment, short of cash, and far from home, he was befriended by Catherine Greene. Phineas Miller, a young man of Whitney's age, Connecticut-born and Yale-educated, managed Mulberry Grove, Greene's plantation. Miller and Whitney became friends.

At a time when English mills were hungry for cotton, the South exported a small amount of the black-seed, long-staple variety. Though it could easily be cleaned of its seed by passing it through a pair of rollers, its cultivation was limited to the coast. On the other hand, a green-seed, short-staple variety that grew in the interior resisted cleaning; its fiber adhered to the seed. Whitney saw that a machine to clean the green-seed cotton could make the South prosperous and make its inventor rich. He set to work and constructed a crude model. Whitney's cotton gin had four parts: (1) a hopper to feed the cotton into the gin; (2) a revolving cylinder studded with hundreds of short wire hooks, closely set in ordered lines to match fine grooves cut in (3) a stationary breastwork that strained out the seed while the fiber flowed through; and (4) a clearer, which was a cylinder set with bristles, turning in the opposite direction, that brushed the cotton from the hooks and let it fly off by its own centrifugal force.

After perfecting his machine Whitney secured a patent (1794), and he and Miller went into business manufacturing and servicing the new gins. However, the unwillingness of the planters to pay the service costs and the ease with which the gins could be pirated put the partners out of business by 1797.

The planters' ability to defeat lawsuits brought against

them by Whitney for infringement of patent rights and their mounting wealth apparently induced a sense of guilt at denying the inventor any reward: in 1802 the state of South Carolina agreed to pay $50,000, half the sum asked by Miller & Whitney for the patent rights. The action was followed by similar settlements with North Carolina, Tennessee, and, finally and reluctantly, Georgia. Miller & Whitney grossed about $90,000; the partners netted practically nothing. When Congress refused to renew the patent, which expired in 1807, Whitney concluded that "an invention can be so valuable as to be worthless to the inventor." He never patented his later inventions, one of which was a milling machine.

Whitney learned much from his experience. He knew his own competence and integrity, which were acknowledged and respected. He redirected his mechanical and entrepreneurial talents to other projects in which his system for manufacturing gins was applicable. In 1797 the government, threatened by war with France, solicited 40,000 muskets from private contractors because the two national armories had produced only 1,000 muskets in three years. Twenty-six contractors bid for a total of 30,200. Like the government armories, they used the conventional method whereby a skilled workman fashioned a complete musket, forming and fitting each part. Thus, each weapon was unique; if a part broke, its replacement had to be especially made.

Whitney broke with this tradition with a plan to supply 10,000 muskets in two years. He designed machine tools by which an unskilled workman made only a particular part that conformed precisely, as precision was then measured, to a model. The sum of such parts was a musket. Any part would fit any musket of that design. He had grasped the concept of interchangeable parts. "The tools which I contemplate to make," he explained, "are similar to an engraving on copper plate from which may be taken a great number of impressions perceptibly alike."

But more than 10 years passed before Whitney delivered his 10,000 muskets. He constantly had to plead for time while struggling against unforeseen obstacles, such as epidemics and delays in supplies, to create a new system of production. Finally, he overcame most of the skepticism in 1801, when, in Washington, D.C., before President-elect Thomas Jefferson and other officials, he demonstrated the result of his system: from piles of disassembled muskets they picked parts at random and assembled complete muskets. They were the witnesses at the inauguration of the American system of mass production.

In 1817 Whitney married Henrietta Edwards, granddaughter of the Puritan theologian Jonathan Edwards. Of his four children, three survived, including Eli Whitney, Jr., who continued his father's arms manufactory in Hamden, Connecticut.

## ALOIS SENEFELDER

(b. Nov. 6, 1771, Prague [now in the Czech Republic]—d. Feb. 26, 1834, Munich, Ger.)

Johann Nepomuk Franz Alois Senefelder was a German inventor of lithography.

The son of an actor at the Theater Royal in Prague, Senefelder was unable to continue his studies at the University of Ingolstadt after his father's death and thus tried to support himself as a performer and author, but without success. He learned printing in a printing office, purchased a small press, and sought to do his own printing.

Desiring to publish plays that he had written but unable to afford the expensive engraving of printing plates, Senefelder tried to engrave them himself. His work on copper plates was not proving very successful when an accident led to his discovery of the possibilities of stone (1796). Senefelder records that one day he jotted down a laundry list with grease pencil on a piece of Bavarian limestone. It occurred to him that if he etched away the rest of the surface, the markings would be left in relief. Two years of experimentation eventually led to the discovery of flat-surface printing (modern lithography, from Greek *lithos*, "stone"). Senefelder closely held the secret of lithographic printing until 1818, when he documented his discovery in *Vollständiges Lehrbuch der Steindruckerey* (1818; *A Complete Course of Lithography*).

Senefelder later accepted an offer from a music publisher, Johann Anton André, to set himself up at Offenbach and train others in his lithographic process. In later years the king of Bavaria settled a handsome pension on Senefelder.

## SIR WILLIAM CONGREVE

(b. May 20, 1772, London, Eng.—d. May 16, 1828, Toulouse, France)

Sir William Congreve was an English artillery officer and inventor, best known for his military rocket, which was a significant advance on earlier black-powder rockets. It provided the impetus for an early wave of enthusiastic utilization of rockets for military purposes in Europe.

Congreve based his rockets on those used by the Indian prince Hyder Ali against the British in 1792 and 1799 at Seringapatam. In 1805 he built a rocket 40.5 inches (103 cm) long, with a stabilizing stick 16 feet (4.9 m) long and a range of 2,000 yards (1.8 km). Congreve's rockets were used to bombard Boulogne, Copenhagen, and Danzig in the Napoleonic Wars and in the British attack on Fort

McHenry, near Baltimore, in 1814, which inspired Francis Scott Key to write in the "Star Spangled Banner" (now the U.S. national anthem): " . . . the rockets' red glare, the bombs bursting in air."

Congreve continued to improve his rockets' range and accuracy, leading many European countries to form rocket corps, usually attached to artillery units. Performance of the Congreve rockets was poor by modern standards because the only available propellant was black powder, which is not ideal for propulsion. They were made obsolete by improved artillery and ordnance, but they continued to find uses for flares and ship rescue.

Congreve is also usually considered the first modern inventor to propose plating warships with armor (1805) to protect against artillery fire. Upon the death of his father in 1814 (whose baronetcy he inherited), he became comptroller of the Royal Laboratory of Woolwich Arsenal. From 1818 until his death, Congreve was a member of Parliament for Plymouth, Devon.

## RENÉ LAËNNEC

(b. Feb. 17, 1781, Quimper, Brittany, France—d. Aug. 13, 1826, Kerlouanec)

René-Théophile-Hyacinthe Laënnec was a French physician who invented the stethoscope and perfected the art of auditory examination of the chest cavity.

When Laënnec was five years old, his mother, Michelle Félicité Guesdon, died from tuberculosis, leaving Laënnec and his brother, Michaud, in the incompetent care of their father, Théophile-Marie Laënnec, who worked as a civil servant and had a reputation for reckless spending. In 1793, during the French Revolution, Laënnec went to live with his uncle, Guillaume-François Laënnec, in the port city of Nantes, located in the Pays de la Loire region of western France. Laënnec's uncle was the dean of medicine at the University of Nantes. Although the region was in the midst of counterrevolutionary revolts, the young Laënnec settled into his academic training and, under his uncle's direction, began his medical studies. His first experience working in a hospital setting was at the Hôtel-Dieu of Nantes, where he learned to apply surgical dressings and to care for patients. In 1800 Laënnec went to Paris and entered the École Pratique, studying anatomy and dissection in the laboratory of surgeon and pathologist Guillaume Dupuytren. Dupuytren was a bright and ambitious academic who became known for his many surgical accomplishments and for his work in alleviating permanent tissue contracture in the palm, a condition later named Dupuytren contracture. While Dupuytren undoubtedly influenced Laënnec's studies, Laënnec also received instruction from other well-known French anatomists and physicians, including Gaspard Laurent Bayle, who studied tuberculosis and cancer; Marie-François-Xavier Bichat, who helped establish histology, the study of tissues; and Jean-Nicolas Corvisart des Marets, who used chest percussion to assess heart function and who served as personal physician to Napoleon I.

Laënnec became known for his studies of peritonitis, amenorrhea, the prostate gland, and tubercle lesions. He graduated in 1804 and continued his research as a faculty member of the Society of the School of Medicine in Paris. He wrote several articles on pathological anatomy and became devoted to Roman Catholicism, which led to his appointment as personal physician to Joseph Cardinal Fesch, half brother of Napoleon and French ambassador to the Vatican in Rome. Laënnec remained Fesch's physician until 1814, when the cardinal was exiled after Napoleon's empire fell. While Laënnec's embrace of Catholic doctrine was viewed favorably by royalists, many others in the medical profession criticized his conservatism, which contradicted the views of many academicians. Nonetheless, Laënnec's restored faith inspired him to find better ways to care for people, especially the poor. From 1812 to 1813, during the Napoleonic Wars, Laënnec took charge of the wards in the Salpêtrière Hospital in Paris, which was reserved for wounded soldiers. After the return of the monarchy, in 1816 Laënnec was appointed as physician at the Necker Hospital in Paris, where he developed the stethoscope.

Laënnec's original stethoscope design consisted of a hollow tube of wood that was 1.4 inches (3.5 cm) in diameter and 10 inches (25 cm) long and was monoaural, transmitting sound to one ear. It could be easily disassembled and reassembled, and it used a special plug to facilitate the transmission of sounds from the patient's heart and lungs. His instrument replaced the practice of immediate auscultation, in which the physician laid his ear on the chest of the patient to listen to chest sounds. The awkwardness that this method created in the case of women patients compelled Laënnec to find a better way to listen to the chest. His wooden monoaural stethoscope was replaced by models using rubber tubing at the end of the 19th century. Other advancements include the development of binaural stethoscopes, capable of transmitting sounds to both ears of the physician.

In 1819 Laënnec published *De l'auscultation médiate* ("On Mediate Auscultation"), the first discourse on a variety of heart and lung sounds heard through the stethoscope. The first English translation of *De l'auscultation médiate* was published in London in 1821. Laënnec's treatise aroused intense interest, and physicians from throughout Europe came to Paris to learn about Laënnec's diagnostic tool. He became an internationally renowned lecturer. In 1822 Laënnec was appointed chair and professor of medicine at the College of France, and the following year he became a full member of the French Academy of Medicine and a professor at the medical clinic of the Charity Hospital in Paris. In 1824 he was made a chevalier of the Legion of Honor. That same year Laënnec married Jacquette Guichard, a widow. They did not have any children, his wife having suffered a miscarriage. Two years later at the age of 45 Laënnec died from cavitating tuberculosis—the same disease that he helped elucidate using his stethoscope. Using his own invention, he could diagnose himself and understand that he was dying.

Because Laënnec's stethoscope enabled heart and lung sounds to be heard without placing an ear on the patient's chest, the stethoscope technique became known as the "mediate" method for auscultation. Throughout Laënnec's medical work and research, his diagnoses were supported with observations and findings from autopsies. In addition to revolutionizing the diagnosis of lung disorders, Laënnec introduced many terms still used today. For example, *Laënnec's cirrhosis*, used to describe micronodular cirrhosis (growth of small masses of tissue in the liver that cause degeneration of liver function), and *melanose* (Greek, meaning "black"), which he coined in 1804 to describe melanoma. Laënnec was the first to recognize that melanotic lesions were the result of metastatic melanoma, in which cancer cells from the original tumor site spread to other organs and tissues in the body. He is considered the father of clinical auscultation, and he wrote the first descriptions of pneumonia, bronchiectasis, pleurisy, emphysema, and pneumothorax. His classification of pulmonary conditions is still used today.

# GEORGE STEPHENSON

(b. June 9, 1781, Wylam, Northumberland, Eng.—d. Aug. 12, 1848, Chesterfield, Derbyshire)

George Stephenson was an English engineer and principal inventor of the railroad locomotive.

Stephenson was the son of a mechanic who operated a Newcomen atmospheric-steam engine that was used to pump out a coal mine at Newcastle upon Tyne. The boy went to work at an early age and without formal schooling; by age 19 he was operating a Newcomen engine. His curiosity aroused by the Napoleonic war news, he enrolled in night school and learned to read and write. He soon married and, in order to earn extra income, learned to repair shoes, fix clocks, and cut clothes for miners' wives, getting a mechanic friend, the future Sir William Fairbairn, to take over his engine part-time. His genius with steam engines, however, presently won him the post of engine wright (chief mechanic) at Killingworth colliery.

Stephenson's first wife died, leaving him with a young son, Robert, whom he sent to a Newcastle school to learn mathematics; every night when the boy came home, father and son went over the homework together, both learning. In 1813 George Stephenson visited a neighboring colliery to examine a "steam boiler on wheels" constructed by John Blenkinsop to haul coal out of the mines. In the belief that the heavy contraption could not gain traction on smooth wooden rails, Blenkinsop had given it a ratchet wheel running on a cogged third rail, an arrangement that created frequent breakdowns. Stephenson thought he could do better, and, after conferring with Lord Ravensworth, the principal owner of Killingworth, he built the *Blucher*, an engine that drew eight loaded wagons carrying 30 tons of coal at 4 miles (6 km) per hour. Not satisfied, he sought to improve his locomotive's power and introduced the "steam blast," by which exhaust steam was redirected up the chimney, pulling air after it and increasing the draft. The new design made the locomotive truly practical.

Over the next few years, Stephenson built several locomotives for Killingworth and other collieries and gained a measure of fame by inventing a mine-safety lamp. In 1821 he heard of a project for a railroad, employing draft horses, to be built from Stockton to Darlington to facilitate exploitation of a rich vein of coal. At Darlington he interviewed the promoter, Edward Pease, and so impressed him that Pease commissioned him to build a steam locomotive for the line. On September 27, 1825, railroad transportation was born when the first public passenger train, pulled by Stephenson's *Active* (later renamed *Locomotion*), ran from Darlington to Stockton, carrying 450 persons at 15 miles (24 km) per hour. Liverpool and Manchester interests called him in to build a 40-mile (64 km) railroad line to connect the two cities. To survey and construct the line, Stephenson had to outwit the violent hostility of farmers and landlords who feared, among other things, that the railroad would supplant horse-drawn transportation and shut off the market for oats.

When the Liverpool-Manchester line was nearing completion in 1829, a competition was held for locomotives; Stephenson's new engine, the *Rocket*, which he built with his son, Robert, won with a speed of 36 miles (58 km) per hour. Eight locomotives were used when the Liverpool-Manchester line opened on September 15, 1830, and all of them had been built in Stephenson's Newcastle works. From this time on, railroad building spread rapidly throughout Britain, Europe, and North America, and George Stephenson continued as the chief guide of the revolutionary transportation medium, solving problems of roadway construction, bridge design, and locomotive and rolling-stock manufacture. He built many other railways in the Midlands, and he acted as consultant on many railroad projects at home and abroad.

## LOUIS DAGUERRE

(b. Nov. 18, 1787, Cormeilles, near Paris, France—d. July 10, 1851, Brysur-Marne)

Louis-Jacques-Mandé Daguerre, a French painter and physicist, invented the first practical process of photography, known as the daguerreotype. Though the first permanent photograph from nature was made in 1826/27 by Nicéphore Niépce of France, it was of poor quality and required about eight hours' exposure time. The process that Daguerre developed required only 20 to 30 minutes.

*Louis-Jacques-Mandé Daguerre*

Daguerre was at first an inland revenue officer and then a scene painter for the opera. Between 1822 and 1839 he was coproprietor of the Diorama in Paris, an auditorium in which he and his partner Charles-Marie Bouton displayed immense paintings, 45.5 by 71.5 feet (14 by 22 m) in size, of famous places and historical events. A similar establishment that he opened in

Regent's Park, London, was destroyed by fire in 1839. The partners painted the scenes on translucent paper or muslin and, by the careful use of changing lighting effects, were able to present vividly realistic tableaux. The views provided grand and illusionistic entertainment, and the amazing trompe l'oeil effect was purposely heightened by the accompaniment of appropriate music and the positioning of real objects, animals, or people in front of the painted scenery.

Like many other artists of his time, Daguerre made preliminary sketches by tracing the images produced by both the camera obscura and the camera lucida, a prism-fitted instrument that was invented in 1807. His attempt to retain the duplication of nature he perceived in the camera obscura's ground glass led in 1829 to a partnership with Niépce, with whom he worked in person and by correspondence for the next four years (Niépce died in 1833). However, Daguerre's interest was in shortening the exposure time necessary to obtain an image of the real world, while Niépce remained interested in producing reproducible plates. It appears that by 1835 Daguerre had discovered that a latent image forms on a plate of iodized silver and that it can be "developed" and made visible by exposure to mercury vapor, which settles on the exposed parts of the image. Exposure times could thus be reduced from eight hours to 30 minutes. The results were not permanent, however; when the developed picture was exposed to light, the unexposed areas of silver darkened until the image was no longer visible. By 1837 Daguerre was able to fix the image permanently by using a solution of table salt to dissolve the unexposed silver iodide. That year he produced a photograph of his studio on a silvered copper plate, a photograph that was remarkable for its fidelity and detail. Also that year, Niépce's son Isidore signed an agreement with Daguerre affirming Daguerre as the inventor of a new process, "the daguerreotype."

On January 9, 1839, a full description of Daguerre's process was announced at a meeting of the Academy of Sciences by the eminent astronomer and physicist François Arago. On August 19 full working details were published. Daguerre wrote a booklet describing the process, *An Historical and Descriptive Account of the Various Processes of the Daguerreotype and the Diorama*, which at once became a best seller; 29 editions and translations appeared before the end of 1839. Also in 1839 Daguerre and the heir of Niépce were assigned annuities of 6,000 francs and 4,000 francs, respectively, in return for their photographic process. Daguerre was appointed an officer of the Legion of Honor.

## SAMUEL F. B. MORSE

(b. April 27, 1791, Charlestown, Mass., U.S.—d. April 2, 1872, New York, N.Y.)

Samuel Finley Breese Morse was an American painter and inventor who, independent of similar efforts in Europe, developed an electric telegraph (1832–35). In 1838 he developed the Morse code.

Morse was the son of Jedidiah Morse, the distinguished geographer and Congregational clergyman. From Phillips Academy in Andover, where he had been an unsteady and eccentric student, his parents sent him to Yale College. Although an indifferent scholar, his interest was aroused by lectures on the then little-understood subject of electricity. To the distress of his austere parents, he also enjoyed painting miniature portraits.

After graduating from Yale in 1810, Morse became a clerk for a Boston book publisher. But painting continued

Fig. 3225.

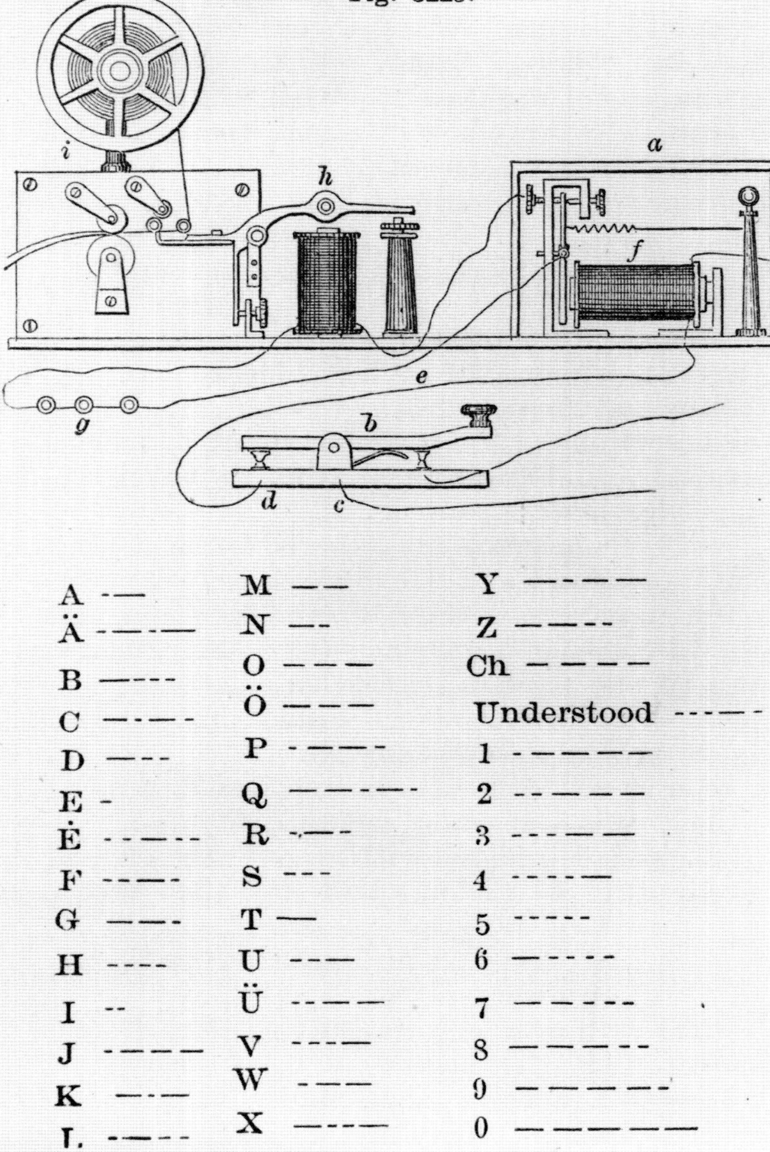


*Morse Apparatus and Alphabet.*

*This print shows the machines used for sending and receiving coded telegraph messages, as well as the alphabet for Morse code.*

to be his main interest, and in 1811 his parents helped him to go to England in order to study that art. During the War of 1812, between Great Britain and the United States, Morse reacted to the English contempt for Americans by becoming passionately pro-American. Like the majority of Americans of his time, however, he accepted English artistic standards, including the "historical" style of painting—the romantic portrayal of legends and historical events with personalities gracing the foreground in grand poses and brilliant colors.

But when, on his return home in 1815, Morse found that Americans did not appreciate his historical canvases, he reluctantly took up portraiture again to earn a living. He began as an itinerant painter in New England, New York, and South Carolina; after 1825, on settling in New York City, he painted some of the finest portraits ever done by an American artist. He combined technical competence and a bold rendering of his subjects' character with a touch of the Romanticism he had imbibed while he was in England.

Although often poor during those early years, Morse was sociable and at home with intellectuals, the wealthy, the religiously orthodox, and the politically conservative. In addition, he possessed the gift of friendship. Among his friends in his middle years were the French hero of the American Revolution, the marquis de Lafayette, whose attempts to promote liberal reform in Europe Morse ardently endorsed, and the novelist James Fenimore Cooper. Morse and Cooper shared several traits: both were ardent U.S. republicans, though both had aristocratic social tastes, and both suffered from the American preference for European art.

Morse also had the gift of leadership. As part of a campaign against the licentiousness of the theater, he helped launch, in 1827, the New York *Journal of Commerce*, which refused theater advertisements. He also was a founder of the National Academy of Design, organized to increase U.S. respect for painters, and was its first president from 1826 to 1845.

In 1832, while returning by ship from studying art in Europe, Morse conceived the idea of an electric telegraph as the result of hearing a conversation about the newly discovered electromagnet. Although the idea of an electric telegraph had been put forward before 1800, Morse believed that his was the first proposal. He probably made his first working model by 1835. Meanwhile, he was still devoting most of his time to painting, teaching art at the University of the City of New York (later New York University), and to politics. But, by 1837, he turned his full attention to the new invention. A colleague at the university showed him a detailed description of an alternative model proposed in 1831, and a friend offered to provide materials and labor to build models in his family's ironworks. These two became partners in Morse's telegraph rights. By 1838 he had developed the system of dots and dashes that became known throughout the world as the Morse code. In 1838, while unsuccessfully attempting to interest Congress in building a telegraph line, he acquired a congressman as an additional partner. After failing to organize the construction of a Morse line in Europe, Morse was finally able to obtain, without his partners' cooperation, financial support from Congress for the first telegraph line in the United States, from Baltimore to Washington. In 1844 the line was completed, and he sent the first message, "What hath God wrought!"

Morse was immediately involved in legal claims by his partners and by rival inventors. He fought vigorously in this dispute, and a series of legal battles culminating in a U.S. Supreme Court decision established his patent rights in 1854. As telegraph lines lengthened on both sides of the

Atlantic, his wealth and fame increased. By 1847 Morse had bought Locust Grove, an estate overlooking the Hudson River near Poughkeepsie, New York, where, early in the 1850s, he built an Italian villa-style mansion. He spent his summers there with his large family of children and grandchildren, returning each winter season to his brownstone home in New York City.

In his old age, Morse, a patriarch with a flowing beard, became a philanthropist. He gave generously to Vassar College, of which he was a founder and trustee; to his alma mater, Yale College; and to churches, theological seminaries, Bible societies, mission societies, and temperance societies, as well as to poor artists.

Even during Morse's own lifetime, the world was much changed by the telegraph. After his death in 1872, his fame as the inventor of the telegraph was obscured by the invention of the telephone, radio, and television. Meanwhile his reputation as an artist has grown. At one time he did not wish to be remembered as a portrait painter, but his powerful and sensitive portraits, among them those of Lafayette, the American writer William Cullen Bryant, and other prominent men, have been exhibited throughout the United States. His 1837 telegraph instrument is preserved by the Smithsonian Institution's National Museum of American History in Washington, D.C., while his estate, Locust Grove, is now designated a historic landmark.

## CHARLES BABBAGE

(b. Dec. 26, 1791, London, Eng.—d. Oct. 18, 1871, London)

Charles Babbage, an English mathematician and inventor, is credited with having conceived the first automatic digital computer.

In 1812 Babbage helped found the Analytical Society,

whose object was to introduce developments from the European continent into English mathematics. In 1816 he was elected a fellow of the Royal Society of London. He was instrumental in founding the Royal Astronomical (1820) and Statistical (1834) societies. In the meantime (1828–39) he served as Lucasian Professor of Mathematics at the University of Cambridge.

As a founding member of the Royal Astronomical Society, Babbage had seen a clear need to design and build a mechanical device that could automate long, tedious astronomical calculations. He began by writing a letter in 1822 to Sir Humphry Davy, president of the Royal Society, about the possibility of automating the construction of mathematical tables—specifically, logarithm tables for use in navigation. He then wrote a paper, "On the Theoretical Principles of the Machinery for Calculating Tables," which he read to the society later that year. (It won the Royal Society's first Gold Medal in 1823.) Tables then in use often contained errors, which could be a life-and-death matter for sailors at sea, and Babbage argued that, by automating the production of the tables, he could assure their accuracy. Having gained support in the society for his Difference Engine, as he called it, Babbage next turned to the British government to fund development, obtaining one of the world's first government grants for research and technological development.

Babbage approached the project very seriously: he hired a master machinist, set up a fireproof workshop, and built a dustproof environment for testing the device. Up until then calculations were rarely carried out to more than six digits; Babbage planned to produce 20- or 30-digit results routinely. The Difference Engine was a digital device: it operated on discrete digits rather than smooth quantities, and the digits were decimal (0–9), represented by positions on toothed wheels, rather than binary digits, or "bits." When one of the toothed wheels turned from 9 to 0, it caused the next wheel to advance one position, carrying the digit.

The Difference Engine was more than a simple calculator, however. It mechanized not just a single calculation but a whole series of calculations on a number of variables to solve a complex problem. It went far beyond calculators in other ways as well. Like modern computers, the Difference Engine had storage—that is, a place where data could be held temporarily for later processing—and it was designed to stamp its output into soft metal, which could later be used to produce a printing plate.

Nevertheless, the Difference Engine performed only one operation. The operator would set up all of its data registers with the original data, and then the single operation would be repeatedly applied to all of the registers, ultimately producing a solution. Still, in complexity and audacity of design, it dwarfed any calculating device then in existence.

The full engine, designed to be room-sized, was never built, at least not by Babbage. Although he received several government grants, they were sporadic—governments changed, funding often ran out, and he had to personally bear some of the financial costs—and he was working at or near the tolerances of the construction methods of the day and ran into numerous construction difficulties. All design and construction ceased in 1833, when Joseph Clement, the machinist responsible for actually building the machine, refused to continue unless he was prepaid. (Between 1985 and 2002 British computer scientists built Difference Engine No. 2, a replica faithful to Babbage's original specifications. The completed engine is on permanent exhibit at the Science Museum in London.)

## The Analytical Engine

While working on the Difference Engine, a simpler calculating machine commissioned by the British government, Babbage began to imagine ways to improve it. Chiefly he thought about generalizing its operation so that it could perform other kinds of calculations. By the time funding ran out for his Difference Engine in 1833, he had conceived of something far more revolutionary: a general-purpose computing machine called the Analytical Engine.

The Analytical Engine was to be a general-purpose, fully program-controlled, automatic mechanical digital computer. It would be able to perform any calculation set before it. There is no evidence that anyone before Babbage had ever conceived of such a device, let alone attempted to build one. The machine was designed to consist of four components: the mill, the store, the reader, and the printer. These components are the essential components of every computer today. The mill was the calculating unit, analogous to the central processing unit (CPU) in a modern computer; the store was where data were held prior to processing, exactly analogous to memory and storage in today's computers; and the reader and printer were the input and output devices.

As with the Difference Engine, the project was far more complex than anything theretofore built. The store was to be large enough to hold 1,000 50-digit numbers; this was larger than the storage capacity of any computer built before 1960. The machine was to be steam-driven and run by one attendant. The printing capability was also ambitious, as it had been for the Difference Engine: Babbage wanted to automate the process as much as possible, right up to producing printed tables of numbers.

The reader was another new feature of the Analytical

Engine. Data (numbers) were to be entered on punched cards, using the card-reading technology of the Jacquard loom. Instructions were also to be entered on cards, another idea taken directly from Joseph-Marie Jacquard. The use of instruction cards would make it a programmable device and far more flexible than any machine then in existence. Another element of programmability was to be its ability to execute instructions in other than sequential order. It was to have a kind of decision-making ability in its conditional control transfer, also known as conditional branching, whereby it would be able to jump to a different instruction depending on the value of some data. This extremely powerful feature was missing in many of the early computers of the 20th century.

By most definitions, the Analytical Engine was a real computer as understood today—or would have been, had Babbage not run into implementation problems again. Actually building his ambitious design was judged infeasible given the current technology, and Babbage's failure to generate the promised mathematical tables with his Difference Engine had dampened enthusiasm for further government funding. Indeed, it was apparent to the British government that Babbage was more interested in innovation than in constructing tables.

All the same, Babbage's Analytical Engine was something new under the sun. Its most revolutionary feature was the ability to change its operation by changing the instructions on punched cards. Until this breakthrough, all the mechanical aids to calculation were merely calculators or, like the Difference Engine, glorified calculators. The Analytical Engine, although not actually completed, was the first machine that deserved to be called a computer. Babbage worked on the machine until his death. His design was forgotten until his unpublished notebooks were discovered in 1937.

Babbage made notable contributions in other areas as well. He assisted in establishing the modern postal system in England and compiled the first reliable actuarial tables. He also invented a type of speedometer and the locomotive cowcatcher. It was Babbage who first suggested that the weather of years past could be read from tree rings. He also had a lifelong fascination with keys, ciphers, and mechanical dolls.

## SIR ROWLAND HILL

(b. Dec. 3, 1795, Kidderminster, Worcestershire, Eng.—d. Aug. 27, 1879, Hampstead, London)

Rowland Hill, knighted Sir Rowland in 1860, was an English administrator and educator and the originator of the penny postage system. He is principally known for his development of the modern postal service, which was subsequently adopted throughout the world.

The son of an English schoolmaster, Hill was interested in problems of teaching; for about 15 years he operated schools in which he emphasized student democracy, rigid self-discipline, and intensive teaching. His wide-ranging interests included printing, astronomy, mathematics, and transportation.

Hill's proposals for postal reform were formulated between 1835 and 1837 and were based on the notion that revenue derived from taxes should increase with the growth of the population and national prosperity. In 1837 he published *Post Office Reform: Its Importance and Practicability*, which is justly regarded as one of the most important milestones in postal progress. Based on an exhaustive study of the cost structure of postal operations, it demonstrated conclusively that conveyance charges were an insignificant factor in the total cost of handling a letter. The then current intricate charging scales based on distance were shown to be irrelevant: they inflated operating costs by requiring a host of clerks to apply them and to prepare complicated interoffice accounts. He also realized that another major item in the current cost structure—the collection of money payments on delivery—was easily avoidable. Hill's solution was a uniform rate of postage, regardless of distance, and prepayment of postage by means of adhesive stamps sold by the post office. Hill proposed a basic rate of one penny for each half ounce, calculating the "natural cost of distribution" to be slightly less than this. The cheapest current rate of postage was fourpence, and the average charge 6 1/4 pence (11.56 cents).

Not surprisingly, Hill's proposals rapidly gained strong support: popular agitation for the "penny post" overcame initial political disinterest—and bureaucratic hostility—and the uniform rate and a system of prepayment by stamps were introduced in 1840. The originality of Hill's proposal for an adhesive postage stamp has been questioned but is irrelevant in considering the overall merits of his work. The significance of his reforms lies not only in the fact that they brought the post within the means of the mass of the people but also in the less obvious way in which they gave the postal system the technical capacity to deal with the vastly increased demand for postal service that ensued. The radical simplification of postal organization and methods characterizing Hill's reforms are the key to the speed and economy with which modern postal systems in many countries now handle tens of millions of letters daily.

The chief features of Hill's system were gradually adopted in varying degrees by other countries throughout the world, first among which were Switzerland and Brazil in 1843.

## CHARLES GOODYEAR

(b. Dec. 29, 1800, New Haven, Conn., U.S.—d. July 1, 1860, New York City)

Charles Goodyear was an American inventor whose vulcanization process made possible the commercial use of rubber. Though subsequent discoveries have refined Goodyear's original techniques, the vulcanization process remains fundamentally the same as it was in his day.

Goodyear began his career as a partner in his father's hardware business, which went bankrupt in 1830. He then became interested in discovering a method of treating india rubber so that it would lose its adhesiveness and susceptibility to extremes of heat and cold. He developed a nitric acid treatment and in 1837 contracted for the manufacture by this process of mailbags for the U.S. government, but the rubber fabric proved useless at high temperatures.

For the next few years he worked with Nathaniel M. Hayward (1808–65), a former employee of a rubber factory in Roxbury, Massachusetts, who had discovered that rubber treated with sulfur was not sticky. Goodyear bought Hayward's process. In 1839 he accidentally dropped some India rubber mixed with sulfur on a hot stove and so discovered vulcanization (after Vulcan, the Roman god of fire). Goodyear found that a mixture of rubber with about 8 percent by weight of sulfur and some white lead as an accelerant was transformed, on heating, to an elastic solid that remained elastic and resilient at high temperatures and yet stayed soft at low temperatures. It is now known that sulfur atoms react to form interlinks between the long, chainlike rubber molecules, making a loose molecular network. The original rubber liquid is thus converted into a solid that will not flow even when warm because the molecules are now permanently tied together. Moreover, the addition of a small amount of sulfur in various forms makes the rubber molecules sufficiently irregular that crystallization (and, hence, hardening at low temperatures) is greatly impeded.

Goodyear was granted his first patent in 1844 but had to fight numerous infringements in court; the decisive victory did not come until 1852. That year he went to England, where articles made under his patents had been displayed at the International Exhibition of 1851; while there he unsuccessfully attempted to establish factories. He also lost his patent rights there and in France because of technical and legal problems. In France a company that manufactured vulcanized rubber by his process failed, and in December 1855 Goodyear was imprisoned for debt in Paris. Meanwhile, in the United States, his patents continued to be infringed upon. Although his invention made millions for others, at his death he left debts of some $200,000. He wrote an account of his discovery entitled *Gum-Elastic and Its Varieties* (2 vol.; 1853–55).

## JOHN DEERE

(b. Feb. 7, 1804, Rutland, Vt., U.S.—d. May 17, 1886, Moline, Ill.)

John Deere was a pioneer American inventor and manufacturer of agricultural implements.

Apprenticed to a blacksmith at age 17, Deere set up his own smithy trade four years later and, for 12 years, did work in various towns of his native Vermont. In 1837, when 33 years old, he headed west and eventually settled in Grand Detour, Illinois, where he set up a blacksmith's shop, and sent for his wife and children the following year. He joined in a partnership with Major Leonard Andrus.

In his work, Deere found, through the frequent repairs that he had to make, that the wood and cast-iron plow, used in the sandy soils of the eastern United States from the 1820s, was not suited to the heavy, sticky soils of the prairies. Calculating that an answer lay in an all-steel one-piece share and moldboard, he began experimenting, and by 1838 he and his partner had sold three newly fashioned plows. He kept experimenting, producing 10 improved plows in 1839 and 40 new plows in 1840. By 1846 the annual output was about a thousand plows. Deciding that Grand Detour was not well situated in regard to transportation and resources, Deere sold his interest in the shop to Andrus in 1847 and moved to Moline, Illinois. There he began using imported English steel with great success and soon negotiated with Pittsburgh manufacturers for the development of comparable steel plate. By 1857 Deere's annual output of plows had risen to 10,000.

In 1858 Deere took his son Charles into partnership and in 1863 his son-in-law, Stephen H. Velie; in 1868 the firm was incorporated as Deere & Company. Deere remained president of the company for the rest of his life. Gradually Deere & Company began manufacturing cultivators and other agricultural implements. It is still a major American manufacturer of farm machinery and industrial equipment. Still headquartered in Moline, Ill., it witnessed five generations of Deere family leadership from its inception until 1982.

## CLAUDE-ÉTIENNE MINIÉ

(b. Feb. 13, 1804, Paris, France—d. Dec. 14, 1879, Paris)

Claude-Étienne Minié was a French army officer who solved the problem of designing a bullet for the muzzle-loading rifle. The bullet became known as the Minié ball.

After serving in several African campaigns in the Chasseurs, Minié rose to the rank of captain. In the 1840s he applied himself to the problem of rifled weapons. As killing machines, the old smoothbore infantry muskets were relatively inefficient. Their heavy, round lead balls delivered lethal blows when they hit a human body, but beyond 75 yards (68 m) even trained infantrymen found it difficult to hit an individual adversary, and at 300 yards (274 m) balls from muzzle-loaders lost most of their lethality. These ballistic shortcomings were a product of the requirement that the projectile, in order to be quickly rammed from muzzle to breech, had to fit loosely in the barrel. When discharged, it wobbled down the barrel, contributing to erratic flight after it left the muzzle. Rifled barrels, in which spiral grooves were cut into the bore, were known to improve accuracy by imparting a gyroscopic spin to the projectile, but reloading rifled weapons was slowed because the lead ball had to be driven into the barrel's rifling. In 1826 Henri-Gustave Delvigne of France, seeking a means of expanding the projectile without making it difficult to ram home, created a narrow powder chamber at the breech end of the barrel against which a loosely fitting lead ball came to rest. Ramrod blows expanded the soft lead at the mouth of the chamber so that, when fired, the bullet fit the rifling tightly. In 1844 another French officer, Louis-Étienne de Thouvenin, introduced yet a better method for expanding bullets. His carabine à tige embodied a post or pillar (tige) at the breech against which the bullet was expanded.

These rifles worked better than earlier types, but their deformed balls flew with reduced accuracy. Minié, inspired by Delvigne's later work with cylindrical bullets, designed longer, smaller-diameter projectiles, which, having the same weight as larger round balls, possessed greater cross-sectional density and therefore retained their velocity better. In order to combat the tendency of muzzle-loading rifles to become difficult to load as gunpowder residue collected in the barrels, Minié suggested a major simplification—eliminating the pillar of Thouvenin's weapons and employing in its place a hollow-based bullet with an iron expander plug that caused the projectile to engage the rifling when the weapon was fired. This new projectile could be loaded into dirty rifles with ease, and, because it was not deformed while loading, it had greater accuracy.

Officials in several countries, notably Britain and the United States, saw the significance of Minié's invention. In the Crimean War (1854–56), Russian troops armed with smoothbore muskets were no match for Britons shooting Minié balls from rifled muskets. Massed formations were easy prey, as were cavalry and artillery units. A correspondent for the *Times* of London wrote: "The Minié is king of weapons . . . the volleys of the Minié cleft [Russian soldiers] like the hand of the Destroying Angel." The American Civil War, in which both sides fielded Minié-type infantry weapons, clearly demonstrated the deadly effect of rifled muskets, although many battlefield commanders only slowly appreciated the changing nature of warfare. Individual soldiers could hit their opposing numbers with accurate fire out to 250 yards (223 m), so that frontal assaults, in which soldiers advanced in neat ranks across open fields, had to be abandoned. By 1862 both sides were building field entrenchments and barricades to provide protection from rifle and artillery fire.

Minié was rewarded by the French government with 20,000 francs and an appointment to the staff of the military school at Vincennes. After retiring in 1858 with the rank of colonel, he served as a military instructor for the khedive of Egypt and as a manager at the Remington Arms Company in the United States.

## LOUIS BRAILLE

(b. Jan. 4, 1809, Coupvray, near Paris, France—d. Jan. 6, 1852, Paris)

Louis Braille was a French educator who developed a system of printing and writing that is extensively used by the blind and that was named for him.

Braille was himself blinded at the age of three in an accident that occurred while he was playing with tools in his father's harness shop. A tool slipped and plunged into his right eye. Sympathetic ophthalmia and total blindness followed. Nevertheless, he became a notable musician and excelled as an organist. Upon receiving a scholarship, he went to Paris in 1819 to attend the National Institute for Blind Children, and from 1826 he taught there.

*Louis Braille's language system enables blind people to read; they memorize the meaning of patterns of raised dots and interpret them with their fingers.*

Braille became interested in a system of writing, exhibited at the school by Charles Barbier, in which a message coded in dots symbolizing phonetic sounds was embossed on cardboard. It was called night writing and was intended for nighttime battlefield communications. In 1824, when he was only 15 years old, Braille worked out an adaptation, written with a simple instrument, that met the needs of the sightless. He later took this system, which consists of a six-dot code in various combinations, and adapted it to musical notation. He published a treatise on his type system in 1829, and in 1837 he published a three-volume Braille edition of a popular history schoolbook.

During the last years of his life Braille was ill with tuberculosis. His system had been immediately accepted and used by his fellow students, but wider acceptance was slow in coming. The system was not officially adopted by the school in Paris until 1854, two years after Braille's death. A universal Braille code for the English-speaking world was not adopted until 1932, when representatives from agencies for the blind in Great Britain and the United States met in London and agreed upon a system known as Standard English Braille, grade 2. In 1957 Anglo-American experts again met in London to further improve the system. A century after his death, Braille's remains (minus his hands, which were kept in his birthplace of Coupvray) were moved to Paris for burial in the Panthéon.

## CYRUS McCORMICK

(b. Feb. 15, 1809, Rockbridge county, Va., U.S.—d. May 13, 1884, Chicago, Ill.)

Cyrus Hall McCormick, an American industrialist and inventor, is generally credited with the development (from 1831) of the mechanical reaper.

McCormick was the eldest son of Robert McCormick,

a farmer, blacksmith, and inventor. McCormick's education, in local schools, was limited. Reserved, determined, and serious-minded, he spent nearly all of his time in his father's workshop.

The elder McCormick had invented several practical farm implements but, like other inventors in the United States and England, had failed in his attempt to build a successful reaping machine. In 1831 Cyrus, aged 22, tried his hand at building a reaper. Resembling a two-wheeled, horse-drawn chariot, the machine consisted of a vibrating cutting blade, a reel to bring the grain within its reach, and a platform to receive the falling grain. The reaper embodied the principles that became essential to all subsequent grain-cutting machines.

For farmers in the early 19th century, harvesting required a large number of laborers, and, if they could be found, the cost of hiring them was high. When McCormick's reaper was tested on a neighbor's farm in 1831, it offered the hope that the yield of the farmer's fields would soon not be limited to the amount of labor available. The machine had defects, not the least of which was a clatter so loud that people were required to walk alongside to calm the frightened horses.

McCormick took out a patent in 1834, but his chief interest at that time was the family's iron foundry. When the foundry failed in the wake of the Bank Panic of 1837, leaving the family deeply in debt, McCormick turned to his still-unexploited reaper and improved it. He sold two reapers in 1841, seven in 1842, 29 in 1843, and 50 the following year.

An 1844 visit to the prairie states in the Midwest convinced McCormick that the future of his reaper and of the world's wheat production lay in this vast fertile land rather than in the rocky, hilly East. In 1847, with further patented improvements, he opened a factory in the then small, swampy, lakeside town of Chicago in partnership with the mayor, William Ogden, who capitalized the venture with $50,000 of his own money. The first year, 800 machines were sold. More were sold the next year, and McCormick was able to buy out Ogden.

McCormick's main rival was Obed Hussey, whose machine proved to be inferior as a reaper but superior as a mower. When McCormick's basic patent expired in 1848, competing manufacturers—Hussey among them—tried to block renewal. The ensuing legal battle was but one of many in McCormick's career. He was involved in endless litigation not only with rival manufacturers and infringers but also with the New York Central Railroad, which he sued for $20,000 damages following an altercation over an $8.75 overcharge on his wife's baggage. He fought this particular case up to the Supreme Court three times—and won, even though it took 20 years. He did not win his 1848 patent renewal battle, however. Except for improvements on the reaper patented after 1831, the basic machine passed into the public domain. McCormick then set out to beat his manufacturing competitors another way: by outselling them.

Pockets stuffed with order blanks, McCormick rode over the plains selling his reaper to farmers and would-be farmers. To increase sales, he used innovations such as mass production, advertising, public demonstration, warranty of product, and extension of credit to his customers. Soon the factory expanded, and the company had a traveling sales force. By 1850 the McCormick reaper was known in every part of the United States, and at the Great Exhibition of 1851 in London it was introduced to European farmers. Although mocked by the *Times* of London as "a cross between an Astley Chariot, a wheelbarrow, and a flying machine," the reaper took the Grand Prize. In 1855 it won the Grand Medal of Honor at the Paris International Exposition. There followed a long series of prize honors and awards that made the McCormick reaper known to farmers worldwide.

By 1856 McCormick was selling more than 4,000 machines a year. In the 1858 account of his marriage to Nancy (Nettie) Fowler, the *Chicago Daily Press* referred to him as the "massive Thor of industry." Business did not absorb all of his energy. He also became active in the Democratic Party and in the Presbyterian Church, establishing the McCormick Theological Seminary in Chicago.

In 1871 the Chicago Fire gutted his factory. Then—more than 60 years old, his fortune long since made—he rebuilt. When he died, his business was still growing. In 1902 the McCormick Harvesting Company joined with other companies to form International Harvester Company, with McCormick's son, Cyrus Jr., as its first president.

## ELISHA GRAVES OTIS

(b. Aug. 3, 1811, Halifax, Vt., U.S.—d. April 8, 1861, Yonkers, N.Y.)

Elisha Graves Otis was the American inventor of the safety elevator.

A descendant of a James Otis who emigrated from England to New England in 1631, the young Otis grew up in Vermont and, at age 19, moved to Troy, New York, and later to Brattleboro, Vermont, working at various jobs. From 1838 to 1845, in Brattleboro, he manufactured wagons and carriages and then moved his family to Albany, New York, where, while employed as a master mechanic in a bedstead factory, he invented several labor-saving machines. In 1851 he was in Bergen, New Jersey, again as master mechanic in a bedstead factory. The Bergen firm sent him to Yonkers, New York, in 1852 to operate a new factory and to install its machinery. There he designed and installed what he called the "safety hoist," the first elevator equipped with an automatic safety device to prevent it from falling if the lifting chain or rope broke. Prior to this invention, the poor reliability of the ropes (generally hemp) used at that time made lifting platforms unsatisfactory for passenger use. Otis's device incorporated a clamping arrangement that gripped the guide rails on which the car moved when tension was released from the hoist rope. The next year Otis resigned from his job and set up a small elevator shop in Yonkers, selling his first elevator machine on September 20, 1853. It hauled freight. Orders were few until May 1854, when, at the Crystal Palace in New York City, he demonstrated his elevator by riding the platform high in the air and ordering the rope cut. On March 23, 1857, he installed the first safety elevator for passenger service in the store of E.V. Haughwout & Co. in New York City; driven by steam power, it climbed five stories in less than a minute and was a pronounced success. On January 15, 1861, Otis patented an independently controlled steam engine for elevator use (installed in 1862). This invention laid the foundation for the business that his two sons, Charles and Norton, carried on after his death as owners of what eventually became the Otis Elevator Company.

Otis also devised a number of other mechanical contrivances. In 1852 he patented some railroad-car trucks and brakes. In 1857 he patented a steam plow, and in 1858 he patented a bake oven.

## SIR HENRY BESSEMER

(b. Jan. 19, 1813, Charlton, Hertfordshire, Eng.—d. March 15, 1898, London)

Sir Henry Bessemer was an English inventor and engineer who developed the first process for manufacturing steel inexpensively (1856), leading to the development of the Bessemer converter. He was knighted in 1879.

Bessemer was the son of an engineer and typefounder. He early showed considerable mechanical skill and inventive powers. After the invention of movable stamps for dating deeds and other government documents and the improvement of a typesetting machine, he went to the manufacture of "gold" powder from brass for use in paints. The florid decoration of the time demanded great quantities of such material, and Bessemer's secret process soon brought him great wealth.

He developed other inventions, notably sugarcane-crushing machinery of advanced design, but he was soon devoted to metallurgy. In his time there were but two iron-based construction materials: cast iron made by the treatment of iron ore with coke in the blast furnace and wrought iron made from cast iron in primitive furnaces by the laborious manual process of "puddling" (stirring the melted iron to remove carbon and raking off the slag). Cast iron was excellent for load-bearing purposes, such as columns or bridge piers, and for engine parts, but for girders and other spans, and particularly for rails, only wrought iron was suitable. Puddling removed carbon, which makes cast iron brittle, and produced a material that could be rolled or forged, but only in "blooms," or large lumps of 100–200 pounds (45–90 kg), and that was full of slag. The blooms had to be laboriously forged together by steam hammers before they could be rolled to any useful length or shape. The only material known as steel was made by adding carbon to pure forms of wrought iron, also by slow and discontinuous methods; the material was hard, would take an edge, and was used almost entirely for cutting tools.

During the Crimean War, Bessemer invented an elongated artillery shell that was rotated by the powder gases. The French authorities with whom he was negotiating, however, pointed out that their cast-iron cannon would not be strong enough for this kind of shell. He thereupon attempted to produce a stronger cast iron. In his experiments he discovered that the excess oxygen in the hot gases of his furnace appeared to have removed the carbon from the iron pigs that were being preheated—much as the carbon is removed in a puddling furnace—leaving a skin of pure iron. Bessemer then found that blowing air through melted cast iron not only purified the iron but also heated it further, allowing the purified iron to be easily poured. This heating effect is caused by the reaction of oxygen with the carbon and silicon in the iron. Utilizing these new techniques, which later became known as the Bessemer process, he was soon able to produce large, slag-free ingots as workable as any wrought-iron bloom, and far larger; he invented the tilting converter into which molten pig iron could be poured before air was blown in from below. Eventually, with the aid of an iron-manganese alloy, which was developed at that time by Robert Forester Mushet, Bessemer also found how to remove excess oxygen from the decarburized iron.

His announcement of the process in 1856 before the British Association for the Advancement of Science in Cheltenham, Gloucestershire, brought many ironmasters to his door, and many licenses were granted. Very soon, however, it became clear that two elements harmful to iron, phosphorus and sulfur, were not removed by the process—or at least not by the fireclay lining of Bessemer's converter. It was not until about 1877 that the British metallurgist Sidney Gilchrist Thomas developed a lining that removed phosphorus and made possible the use of phosphoric ores of the Continent.

Bessemer had, unknown to himself, been using phosphorus-free iron, but the ironmasters were not so lucky. Their iron was perfectly satisfactory for the puddling process, in which phosphorus is removed because the temperatures are lower, but it could not be used in the Bessemer process. Bessemer was forced to call in his licenses and find a phosphorus-free source of iron in northwestern England; thus he was able to enter the steel market on his own. Once the phosphorus problem was recognized and solved, he became a licensor once again, and vast profits flowed in. It became clear that "mild steel"—as it was known to distinguish it from the hard tool steels—could more clearly and reliably be used in place of wrought iron for ship plate, girders, sheet, rods, wire, rivets, and other items. The invention of the open-hearth (Siemens-Martin) process in the late 1860s eventually outstripped that of the Bessemer process. This has now yielded place, in great measure, to oxygen steelmaking, which is a further development and refinement of the Bessemer process.

In his later years—the process had not become a clear success until he was nearing 70—Bessemer continued to invent and make discoveries. The solar furnace he built was more than a successful toy; he designed and built an astronomical telescope for his own amusement; and he developed a set of machines for polishing diamonds that helped to reestablish that trade in London.

Apart from his knighthood, he received many honors, such as the Fellowship of the Royal Society. Bessemer's *An Autobiography* (1905), with a concluding chapter by his son, Henry Bessemer, is the only comprehensive biography and the source of most material written about him since.

## SAMUEL COLT

(b. July 19, 1814, Hartford, Conn., U.S.—d. Jan. 10, 1862, Hartford)

Samuel Colt was an American firearms manufacturer who popularized the revolver.

Until the mid-1840s most pistols were single-shot muzzle-loaders fired by wheel lock, flintlock, and percussion ignition systems. Some early pistols, known as "pepperboxes," had several barrels, and as early as the 17th century pistols were manufactured with a revolving chamber to load cartridges successively into a single barrel. However, the principle of the revolving chamber was not used successfully to produce a practical weapon until Colt patented his version.

When Colt was a young seaman, he carved a wooden model of a revolver, and years later he perfected a working version that was patented in England and France in 1835 and in the United States the following year. In the frame of this weapon was a revolving cylinder drilled with several chambers (usually five or six), into which powder and ball (or combustible paper cartridges containing powder and ball) were loaded from the front. In the rear of each chamber a percussion cap was placed over a hollow nipple that directed the jet of flame to the powder when the cap was struck by the hammer. This type of revolver was eventually called "cap-and-ball." Where earlier revolvers required the shooter to line up a chamber with the barrel and cock the hammer in separate steps, Colt devised a single-action mechanical linkage that rotated the cylinder as the hammer was cocked with the thumb.

Colt's single-barreled pistols and rifles were slow to gain acceptance, and a company that formed to manufacture them in Paterson, New Jersey, failed in 1842. The following year he devised an electrically discharged naval mine, the first device using a remotely controlled explosive, and he also conducted a telegraph business that utilized the first underwater cable.

Word from military units that Colt's multi-shot weapons had been effective against Indians in Florida and Texas prompted a government order for 1,000 pistols during the

Mexican War, and Colt resumed firearms manufacture in 1847. In 1855 he opened the world's largest private armory, the Colt's Patent Fire Arms Manufacturing Company, on the banks of the Connecticut River in Hartford. Assisted by Eli Whitney Jr. he developed beyond any industrialist before him the manufacture of interchangeable parts and the production line, and he also applied progressive ideas concerning employee welfare. Colt dominated the manufacture of revolvers until the expiration of his U.S. patent in 1857; his invention made him a wealthy man. His firm produced the pistols most widely used during the American Civil War. Its six-shot, single-action .45-caliber Single Action Army Model 1873, a breech-loading revolver using metallic cartridges, became the most famous sidearm of the West.

## RICHARD J. GATLING

(b. Sept. 12, 1818, Maney's Neck, N.C., U.S.—d. Feb. 26, 1903, New York, N.Y.)

American inventor Richard Jordan Gatling is best known for his invention of the Gatling gun, a crank-operated, multibarrel machine gun, which he patented in 1862.

Gatling's career as an inventor began when he assisted his father in the construction and perfecting of machines for sowing cotton seeds and for thinning cotton plants. In 1839 he perfected a practical screw propeller for steamboats, only to find that a patent had been granted to John Ericsson for a similar invention a few months earlier. He established himself in Saint Louis, Missouri, in 1844, and, taking the cotton-sowing machine as a basis, he adapted it for sowing rice, wheat, and other grains. The introduction of these machines did much to revolutionize the agricultural system in the country.

Becoming interested in the study of medicine during

an attack of smallpox, Gatling completed a course at the Ohio Medical College in 1850. In the same year, he invented a hemp-breaking machine, and in 1857 a steam plow. At the outbreak of the American Civil War he devoted himself at once to the perfecting of firearms. In 1861 he conceived the idea of the rapid-fire machine gun that is associated with his name. After early experiments with a single barrel using paper cartridges (which had a separate percussion cap), he saw in the newly invented brass cartridge (with its own percussion cap) an opportunity to fashion a rapid-fire weapon. Gatling contrived a cluster of 10 barrels, each of which, when rotated by a crank, was loaded and fired once during a complete rotation. The barrels were loaded by gravity and the camming action of the cartridge container, located directly above the gun. Each barrel was loaded and fired during a half-rotation around the central shaft, and the spent cases were ejected during the second half-rotation. By 1862 Gatling had succeeded in perfecting his weapon; but the war was practically over before the federal authorities consented to its official adoption. A few were used by U.S. forces in Cuba in 1898 and in minor military operations around the world. It and all other hand-operated machine guns were made obsolete by truly automatic machine guns, which operated under the energy generated by a fired round. These became militarily effective following the invention of smokeless gunpowder.

## JAMES STARLEY

(b. April 21, 1830, Albourne, Sussex, Eng.—d. June 17, 1881, Coventry, Warwickshire, Eng.)

James Starley was an English inventor whose prolific improvements for bicycles and tricycles earned him the title "Father of the Cycle Trade."

In 1855 Starley moved to London, where he was employed in the manufacture of sewing machines, and two years later he moved to Coventry, where he became managing foreman at the Coventry Sewing Machine Company (later the Coventry Machinists' Company Ltd.). There he invented and patented new models, and many of his features are used in modern sewing machines.

In 1868 Starley became interested in bicycle improvement. At that time the bicycle trade was dominated by French-made velocipedes (*vélocipèdes de pedale*), iron-framed and wooden-wheeled vehicles whose hard ride earned them the sobriquet of "boneshaker"—though innovations such as solid rubber tires and wire-spoked wheels helped to soften the ride. Starley's first bicycle, the Coventry, was quickly followed by the Ariel (1871), notable for its use of center pivot steering. The Ariel had a 48-inch (122 cm) front wheel and a 30-inch (76 cm) rear wheel. Considered the first true bicycle by many historians, the Ariel was the immediate precursor of the high-wheel "ordinary" bicycle and was the standard of bicycle design for the next decade. Starley also invented and manufactured a tangentially spoked wheel, with the spokes connected to the hub at a tangent. His design was a great improvement over radially spoked wheels and is still in use. In 1876 he introduced the highly successful Coventry tricycle and the following year incorporated into it the patented use of the differential gear in conjunction with chain drive.

The ordinary's cranks were directly connected to the front wheel, so that its speed was limited by pedaling cadence and wheel diameter. Larger front wheels went faster and handled better on bad roads, but mounting and dismounting required skill, and the rider sat almost directly over the large front wheel. From that position he could be pitched forward onto his head by road hazards. By the 1890s the term "penny-farthing" had come into use as a pejorative for ordinaries, comparing the front wheel to the large British penny and the rear wheel to the much smaller farthing (quarter-penny). Yet even as the ordinary was developing, numerous designs offered safer alternatives. In 1885 Starley's nephew, John Kemp Starley, designed and manufactured the Rover, regarded as the first successful "safety" bicycle and the prototype of all modern bicycles. The Rover provided all the essential features of the safety bicycle: spoked wheels roughly 30 inches (76 cm) in diameter, a chain-driven rear wheel with the front chainwheel roughly twice as large as the rear sprocket, a low center of gravity, and direct front steering. The design had decisive advantages in stability, braking, and ease of mounting. Prior to 1885 many alternative designs were called safety bicycles, but, after the Rover pattern took over the market in the late 1880s, safety bicycles were simply called bicycles. The last catalog year for ordinaries in England was 1892.

## ALFRED NOBEL

(b. Oct. 21, 1833, Stockholm, Swed.—d. Dec. 10, 1896, San Remo, Italy)

Alfred Bernhard Nobel, a Swedish chemist, engineer, and industrialist, invented dynamite and other, more powerful explosives, but he is also renowned for having founded the Nobel Prizes.

Nobel was the fourth son of Immanuel and Caroline Nobel. Immanuel was an inventor and engineer who had married Caroline Andrietta Ahlsell in 1827. The couple had eight children, of whom only Alfred and three brothers reached adulthood. Alfred was prone to illness as a child, but he enjoyed a close relationship with his mother and displayed a lively intellectual curiosity from an early age. He was interested in explosives, and he learned the fundamentals of engineering from his father. Immanuel, meanwhile, had failed at various business ventures until moving in 1837 to Saint Petersburg in Russia, where he prospered as a manufacturer of explosive mines and machine tools. The Nobel family left Stockholm in 1842 to join the father in Saint Petersburg. Alfred's newly prosperous parents were now able to send him to private tutors, and he proved to be an eager pupil. He was a competent chemist by age 16 and was fluent in English, French, German, and Russian, as well as Swedish.

Alfred Nobel left Russia in 1850 to spend a year in Paris studying chemistry and then spent four years in the United States working under the direction of John Ericsson, the builder of the ironclad warship *Monitor*. Upon his return to Saint Petersburg, Nobel worked in his father's factory, which made military equipment during the Crimean War. After the war ended in 1856, the company had difficulty switching to the peacetime production of steamboat machinery, and it went bankrupt in 1859.

*Today Alfred Nobel is well-known as the founder of the Nobel Prizes, which are highly regarded awards for intellectual achievements.*

Alfred and his parents returned to

Sweden, while his brothers Robert and Ludvig stayed behind in Russia to salvage what was left of the family business. Alfred soon began experimenting with explosives in a small laboratory on his father's estate. At the time, the only dependable explosive for use in mines was black powder, a form of gunpowder. A recently discovered liquid compound, nitroglycerin, was a much more powerful explosive, but it was so volatile that it could not be handled with any degree of safety. Nevertheless, Nobel in 1862 built a small factory to manufacture nitroglycerin, and at the same time he undertook research in the hope of finding a safe way to control the explosive's detonation.

In 1863 he invented a practical detonator consisting of a wooden plug inserted into a larger charge of nitroglycerin held in a metal container; the explosion of the plug's small charge of black powder serves to detonate the much more powerful charge of liquid nitroglycerin. This detonator marked the beginning of Nobel's reputation as an inventor as well as the fortune he was to acquire as a maker of explosives. In 1865 Nobel invented an improved detonator called a blasting cap; it consisted of a small metal cap containing a charge of mercury fulminate that could be exploded by either shock or moderate heat. The invention of the blasting cap inaugurated the modern use of high explosives.

Nitroglycerin itself, however, remained difficult to transport and extremely dangerous to handle. So dangerous, in fact, that Nobel's nitroglycerin factory blew up in 1864, killing his younger brother Emil and several other people. Undaunted by this tragic accident, Nobel built several factories to manufacture nitroglycerin for use in concert with his blasting caps. These factories were as safe as the knowledge of the time allowed, but accidental explosions still occasionally occurred. Nobel's second important invention was that of dynamite in 1867. By chance, he discovered that nitroglycerin was absorbed to dryness by kieselguhr, a porous siliceous earth, and the resulting mixture was much safer to use and easier to handle than nitroglycerin alone. Nobel named the new product dynamite (from Greek *dynamis*, "power") and was granted patents for it in Great Britain (1867) and the United States (1868). Dynamite established Nobel's fame worldwide and was soon put to use in blasting tunnels, cutting canals, and building railways and roads.

In the 1870s and '80s Nobel built a network of factories throughout Europe to manufacture dynamite, and he formed a web of corporations to produce and market his explosives. He also continued to experiment in search of better ones, and in 1875 he invented a more powerful form of dynamite, blasting gelatin, which he patented the following year. Again by chance, he had discovered that mixing a solution of nitroglycerin with a fluffy substance known as nitrocellulose results in a tough, plastic material that has a high water resistance and greater blasting power than ordinary dynamites. In 1887 Nobel introduced ballistite, one of the first nitroglycerin smokeless powders and a precursor of cordite.

Although Nobel held the patents to dynamite and his other explosives, he was in constant conflict with competitors who stole his processes, a fact that forced him into protracted patent litigation on several occasions.

Nobel's brothers Ludvig and Robert, in the meantime, had developed newly discovered oilfields near Baku (now in Azerbaijan) along the Caspian Sea and had themselves become immensely wealthy. Alfred's worldwide interests in explosives, along with his own holdings in his brothers' companies in Russia, brought him a large fortune. In 1893 he became interested in Sweden's arms industry, and the following year he bought an ironworks at Bofors, near Varmland, that became the nucleus of the well-known

Bofors arms factory. Besides explosives, Nobel made many other inventions, such as artificial silk and leather, and altogether he registered more than 350 patents in various countries.

## A Paradoxical Figure

Nobel's complex personality puzzled his contemporaries. Although his business interests required him to travel almost constantly, he remained a lonely recluse who was prone to fits of depression. He led a retired and simple life and was a man of ascetic habits, yet he could be a courteous dinner host, a good listener, and a man of incisive wit. He never married, and apparently preferred the joys of inventing to those of romantic attachment. He had an abiding interest in literature and wrote plays, novels, and poems, almost all of which remained unpublished. He had amazing energy and found it difficult to relax after intense bouts of work. Among his contemporaries, he had the reputation of a liberal or even a socialist, but he actually distrusted democracy, opposed suffrage for women, and maintained an attitude of benign paternalism toward his many employees. Though Nobel was essentially a pacifist and hoped that the destructive powers of his inventions would help bring an end to war, his view of mankind and nations was pessimistic.

By 1895 Nobel had developed angina pectoris, and he died of a cerebral hemorrhage at his villa in San Remo, Italy, in 1896. At his death his worldwide business empire consisted of more than 90 factories manufacturing explosives and ammunition. The opening of his will, which he had drawn up in Paris on November 27, 1895, and had deposited in a bank in Stockholm, contained a great surprise for his family, friends, and the general public. He had always been generous in humanitarian and scientific philanthropies, and he left the bulk of his fortune in trust to establish what came to be the most highly regarded of international awards, the Nobel Prizes.

We can only speculate about the reasons for Nobel's establishment of the prizes that bear his name. He was reticent about himself, and he confided in no one about his decision in the months preceding his death. The most plausible assumption is that a bizarre incident in 1888 may have triggered the train of reflection that culminated in his bequest for the Nobel Prizes. That year Alfred's brother Ludvig had died while staying in Cannes, France. The French newspapers reported Ludvig's death but confused him with Alfred, and one paper sported the headline "Le marchand de la mort est mort" ("The merchant of death is dead.") Perhaps Alfred Nobel established the prizes to avoid precisely the sort of posthumous reputation suggested by this premature obituary. It is certain that the actual awards he instituted reflect his lifelong interest in the fields of physics, chemistry, physiology, and literature. There is also abundant evidence that his friendship with the prominent Austrian pacifist Bertha von Suttner inspired him to establish the prize for peace.

Nobel himself, however, remains a figure of paradoxes and contradictions: a brilliant, lonely man, part pessimist and part idealist, who invented the powerful explosives used in modern warfare but also established the world's most prestigious prizes for intellectual services rendered to humanity.

## JOHN WESLEY HYATT

(b. Nov. 28, 1837, Starkey, N.Y., U.S.—d. May 10, 1920, Short Hills, N.J.)

John Wesley Hyatt, an American inventor and industrialist, discovered the process for making celluloid, the first practical artificial plastic.

As a young man, Hyatt trained as a printer in Illinois and then in Albany, New York. In 1863 he was attracted by a reward of $10,000 offered by a New York billiards company to anyone who could invent a satisfactory substitute for ivory billiard balls. Hyatt experimented with several compositions, none of which produced a successful billiard ball, but he was able to go into business with his brothers making one of the mixtures—a composite of wood pulp and shellac—into embossed checkers and dominoes.

Continuing his experiments, Hyatt found that an attractive and practical plastic material could be made by mixing nitrocellulose (a flammable nitrate of common wood or cotton cellulose), camphor (a waxy resin obtained from Asian camphor trees), and alcohol and then pressing the mixture in a heated mold. The solid solution was kneaded into a doughlike mass to which coloring agents could be added either in the form of dyes for transparent colors or as pigments for opaque colors. The colored mass was rolled, sheeted, and then pressed into blocks. After seasoning, the blocks were sliced; at this point they could be further fabricated, or the sheeting and pressing process could be repeated for various mottled and variegated effects. The plastic, which softened at the temperature of boiling water, could be heated and then pressed into innumerable shapes, and at room temperature it could be sawed, drilled, turned, planed, buffed, and polished.

Hyatt and his brother Isaiah first attempted to market the plastic, which they patented in 1870 as celluloid, as a substitute for hard rubber in denture plates. In 1872 they moved their Celluloid Manufacturing Company from Albany to Newark, New Jersey, where they put numerous patents to work in building up what became the premier celluloid company in the world. The Hyatts concentrated

*John Wesley Hyatt developed the process for making an artificial plastic called celluloid and patented it in 1870.*

on forming celluloid into sheets, rods, and other unfinished shapes, usually leaving their fabrication into practical objects to licensed companies such as the Celluloid Brush Company, the Celluloid Waterproof Cuff and Collar Company, and the Celluloid Piano Key Company.

A tough, flexible, and moldable material, resistant to water, oils, and dilute acids, and capable of low-cost production in a variety of colors, celluloid was made into many other mass-produced goods. In all of these applications celluloid was marketed as an affordable and practical substitute for natural materials such as ivory, tortoise shell, and horn. Beginning in the 1880s celluloid acquired one of its most prominent uses as a substitute for linen in detachable collars and cuffs for men's clothing. Over the years a number of competing plastics were introduced under such fanciful names as Coralline, Ivoride, and Pyralin, and celluloid became a generic term. In 1882 John H. Stevens, a chemist at the Hyatts' company, discovered that amyl acetate was a suitable solvent for diluting celluloid. This allowed the material to be made into clear, flexible film, which other researchers such as Henry Reichenbach of the Eastman Kodak Company further processed into film for still photography and, later, motion pictures. Despite its flammability and tendency to discolor with age, celluloid was virtually unchallenged as the medium for motion pictures until the 1930s, when it began to be replaced by cellulose acetate "safety film." Other disadvantages of celluloid were its tendency to soften under heat and its unsuitability for new, efficient fabrication processes such as injection molding. In the 1920s and '30s celluloid began to be replaced in most of its applications by more versatile materials such as cellulose acetate, Bakelite, and the new vinyl polymers.

In the 1880s the Hyatts set up a company that employed a patented process for purifying water through the use of coagulants and filters. John Hyatt went on to invent a number of new or improved industrial devices, including roller bearings, sugarcane mills, and sewing machines.

## GEORGES LECLANCHÉ

(b. 1839, Paris, France—d. Sept. 14, 1882, Paris)

Georges Leclanché was a French engineer who in about 1866 invented the battery that bears his name. In slightly modified form, the Leclanché cell is produced in great quantities and is widely used in devices such as flashlights and portable radios.

After completing a technical education in 1860, Leclanché began work as an engineer. Six years later he developed his battery, which contained a conducting solution (electrolyte) of ammonium chloride, a negative terminal of zinc, and a positive terminal of manganese dioxide. The Leclanché cell immediately became a commercial success in large sizes because of its readily available low-cost constituent materials.

The original version of the Leclanché cell was actually "wet," as it had an electrolyte consisting of a solution of ammonium chloride. The idea of employing an immobilized electrolyte was finally introduced in the late 1880s and launched the dry-cell industry that continues to flourish today. The Leclanché cell remains the least expensive dry cell and is available nearly everywhere. The anode (negative terminal) of this battery is a zinc alloy sheet or "can," the alloy containing small amounts of lead, cadmium, and mercury. The electrolyte consists of a saturated aqueous solution of ammonium chloride containing roughly 20 percent zinc chloride. The cathode (positive terminal) is made of impure manganese dioxide. This compound is blended with carbon black and electrolyte to create a damp, active cathode mixture which is formed

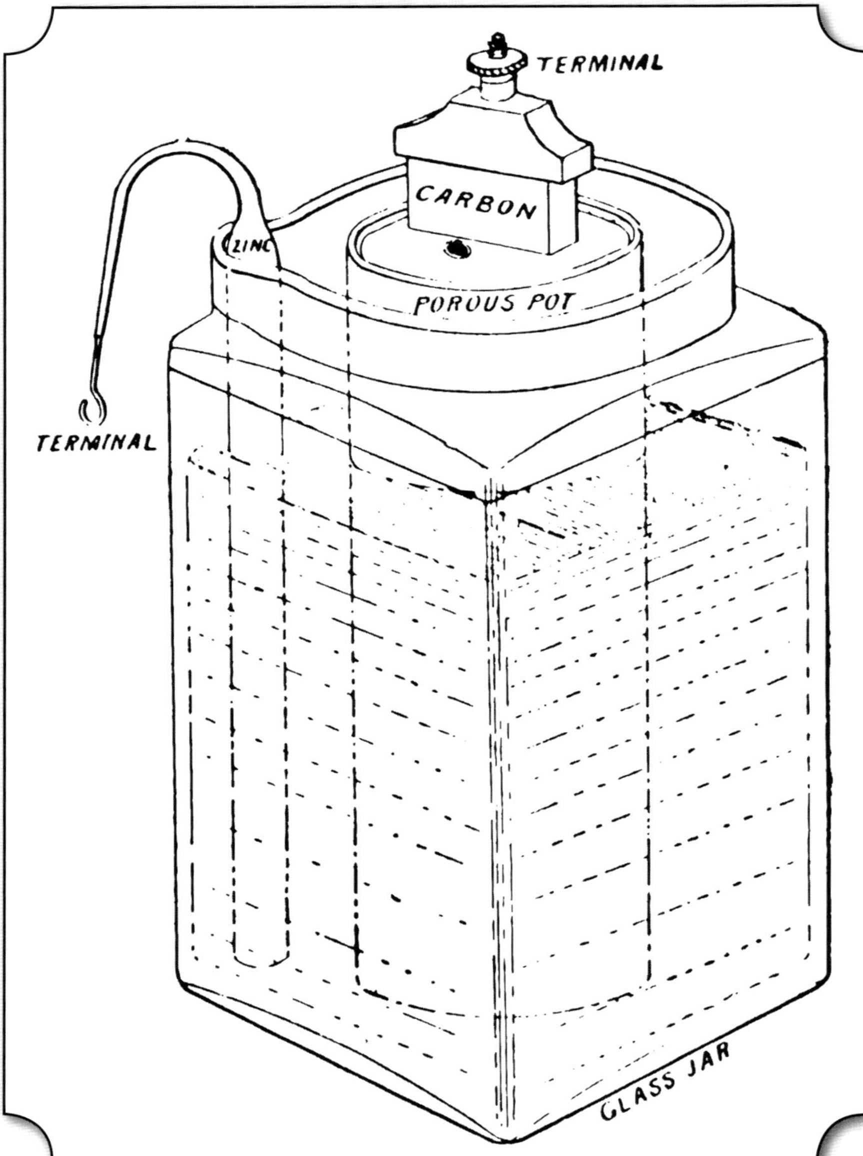


*Georges Leclanché's cell was invented in 1866. This dry cell and its later variations, the zinc chloride and alkaline cells, are batteries commonly used throughout the world.*

around a carbon collector rod, also called an electrode. All batteries of this type are provided with an overwrap structure with metal covers for electrical contact.

In 1867 Leclanché gave up his job to devote full time to his invention; a year later it was adopted by the telegraph service of Belgium. He subsequently opened a factory to produce the battery and other electric devices; the business was taken over by his brother Maurice upon Georges's death in 1882.

# Glossary

**auscultation:** Listening to the body as a method of diagnosis.

**centrifugal:** Moving outward from the center, or directed in such movement.

**coagulant:** A substance that aids a liquid in becoming thicker.

**colliery:** A coal mine.

**lithography:** A printmaking method.

**metallurgy:** The science of the nature and uses of metal.

**paradox:** Having qualities that are opposite.

**patent:** Rights given to a person by the government to make, use, or sell an invention.

**sobriquet:** A nickname.

**tableau:** A scene or sight that looks like a picture.

**treatise:** A formal exposition in writing, generally longer and more specific than an essay.

**trompe l'oeil:** A style of painting that makes the things painted look like real objects.

**vulcanize:** To treat rubber with sulfur and heat to increase its strength and durability.

# FOR MORE INFORMATION

## BOOKS

Coiley, John. *Train*. New York, NY: DK Publishing, 2022.

Kerby, Mona. *Samuel Morse*. Westminster, Maryland: MK Publications, 2020.

Kirkfield, Vivian. *From Here to There: Inventions That Changed the Way the World Moves.* Boston, MA: Houghton Mifflin Harcourt, 2021.

Lucas, Eileen. *Charles Babbage and Ada Lovelace: The Pen Pals Who Imagined the First Computer*. New York, NY: The Rosen Publishing Group, 2021.

## WEBSITES

**Library of Congress: Louis Braille**
*www.loc.gov/nls/new-materials/book-lists/louis-braille-1809-1852/*
Read a brief biography of Louis Braille and find recommendations for books about his life and achievements.

**The Met: Daguerre (1787–1851) and the Invention of Photography**
*www.metmuseum.org/toah/hd/dagu/hd_dagu.htm*
Read more about how Louis Daguerre pioneered the art and science of photography.

**Morse Code Translator**
*https://morsecode.world/international/translator.html*
This website has a translator to change written text into Morse code.

**The Nobel Prize: The Man Behind the Prize**
*www.nobelprize.org/alfred-nobel/*
Learn more about Alfred Nobel, his inventions, and his legacy.

# Index